Healing Scriptures

A Joy-Filled Heart Is Good Medicine

Notes by Jack G. Elder

Copyright © 2015 Jack G. Elder

All rights reserved.

Unless otherwise noted, all scripture references are taken from the *Authorized King James Version* of the Bible. (Updated for reading)

For additional encouragement, see www.jubileeonlinechurch.org.

ISBN-13: 978-1508649359
ISBN-10: 1508649359

CONTENTS

	Preface	Pg. vi
1	Healing in the Old Testament	Pg. 1
2	Healing in The Gospels	Pg. 14
3	Healing in the Early Church	Pg. 43
4	Healing Teaching of the Apostles	Pg. 48
5	Appendix A – Going to the Doctor	Pg. 59
6	Appendix B – Taking Communion	Pg. 61
7	Appendix C – How to Be Saved	Pg. 63

PREFACE

The benefits are plentiful. God's promises are sure. "For all the promises of God in Him *are* yes, and in Him Amen, to the glory of God by us." (2 Corinthians 1:20) Put the healing scriptures in your heart. Read them repeatedly.

Whenever you have a symptom, open up the Word. Read it OUT LOUD. What you read, believe. Thank the Lord for His healing. Take the medicine of the Word every day until the symptoms are gone. Remember it is your faith in God's Word that makes you free. Faith is a response to the love of God for you.

Remember that under the Old Covenant you had to do the law to get your benefits. Under the New Covenant, you get the benefits of healing through believing in the finished work of Jesus. You are not under the law, but under grace. You are highly favored and the whole package is a gift.

As you read these verses, underline or highlight important parts. Find a selection of verses that really speak to you and mark them. Read them morning and evening. Healing is part of your covenant rights through Jesus. Take your healing by faith. Faith is trust. It doesn't mean you have to **do** something. You just have to trust in the finished work of Jesus. That means you must know what the finished worked covers and simply trust in it.

God wants His children well. Jesus came healing all that were sick. Sickness is from the curse that came on man at the fall of Adam. It's a result of giving man's dominion over to Satan. Jesus took it back and gave it to His children.

Faith is not a work that you try to prove to God you deserve healing. Faith flows from knowing you are righteous in Christ and that you are a child of God. If you don't know that you are a child of God, see Appendix C.

I've added a few notes on some of the scriptures. They are just to help you see the wonder of the Word. It is the Word you want filling your heart. It is the Word you want washing over you and renewing your thinking. He sent His word and healed them.

Chapter 1

Healing in the Old Testament

Genesis 20:17
¹⁷ So Abraham prayed to God: and **God healed** Abimelech, and his wife, and his maidservants; and they bore *children*.

This is the first mention in scripture of God healing. Abraham prayed for a heathen king, and God healed him. Even in the Old Testament God is seen as a healing God. It also shows we can pray for anyone's healing whether a believer or not. God hates sickness and disease.

Exodus 15:26
²⁶ …I will put none of these diseases upon you, which I have brought upon the Egyptians: for I *am* the **LORD that heals** you.

God used common diseases of Egypt to make Pharaoh release Israel from the horrific bondage they had under the Egyptians. This promise was to those who obeyed the commandments. That was part of the Old Covenant. The healing blessings were contingent on their obedience.

The New Covenant is contingent on the finished work of Jesus. Healing is in the Cross and our part is to believe in what Jesus has already done—what we will refer to as the "finished work of Jesus." Our healing is found through Jesus. Look to Him. Have faith in His faith. Your healing is not based on how well you obey or how worthy you are. It's based on Jesus alone.

Exodus 23:25, 26

[25] ... and He shall bless your bread, and your water; and **I will take sickness away** from the midst of you. [26] There shall nothing cast their young, nor be barren, in your land: **the number of your days I will fulfil**.

Leviticus 26:4-5

[4] I will give you rain in due season, and the land shall yield her increase, and the trees of the field shall yield their fruit. [5] And your threshing shall reach to the vintage, and the vintage shall reach to the sowing time: and you shall eat your bread to the full, and **dwell in your land safely**.

Numbers 12:13

[13] And Moses cried to the LORD, saying, **Heal** her [Miriam] now, O God, I beseech you.

Deuteronomy 7:14-15

[14] You shall be blessed above all people: there shall not be male or female barren among you, or among your cattle. [15] And the LORD will take away from you **all sickness**, and will put none of the evil diseases of Egypt, which you know, upon you...

You are living in the blessings of God. Remember you are blessed now, through Jesus. God takes away all sickness because of Jesus.

Deuteronomy 11:9
⁹ And that you may **prolong *your* days** in the land, which the LORD swore to your fathers to give to them and to their seed, a land that flows with milk and honey.

Deuteronomy 11:21
²¹ That **your days may be multiplied**, and the days of your children, in the land which the LORD swore to your fathers to give them, as the days of heaven upon the earth.

These verses are your promise of long life and multiplied days on the earth. Receive it by faith and take it by faith. Your illness is not going to shorten it.

Deuteronomy 28:3-13
³ Blessed *shall* you *be* in the city, and blessed *shall* you *be* in the field. ⁴ **Blessed *shall be* the fruit of your body**, and the fruit of your ground, and the fruit of your cattle, the increase of your cattle, and the flocks of your sheep. ⁵ Blessed *shall be* your basket and your store. ⁶ Blessed *shall* you *be* when you come in, and blessed *shall* you *be* when you go out. ⁷ The LORD shall cause your enemies that rise up against you to be smitten before your face: they shall come out against you one way, and flee before you seven ways. ⁸ The LORD shall command the blessing upon you in your storehouses, and in all that you set your hand to; and He shall bless you in the land which the LORD your God gives you. ⁹ The LORD shall establish you a holy people to Himself, as He has sworn to you… ¹¹ And the LORD shall make you plenteous in goods, in the fruit of your body, and in the fruit of your cattle, and in the fruit of your ground, in the land which the LORD swore to your fathers to give you. ¹² The LORD shall open to you His good treasure, the heaven to give the rain to your land in his season, and to bless all the work of your hand:

and you shall lend to many nations, and you shall not borrow. [13] And the LORD shall make you the head, and not the tail; and you shall be above only, and you shall not be beneath…

This is the promise of the blessings. The rest of the chapter contains the curses. But we are not under the curses, because Jesus became a curse for us leaving us with only the blessings. Look at your life as blessed. You are blessed because of Jesus. Keep looking to Jesus, the Author and Finisher of your faith. If you don't feel like you have any faith, look to Jesus who supplies the faith. These blessings are yours through the finished work of Jesus.

Deuteronomy 30:9

[9] And the LORD your God will make you plenteous in every work of your hand, in the **fruit of your body**, and in the fruit of your cattle, and in the fruit of your land, for good: for **the LORD will again rejoice over you for good**, as He rejoiced over your fathers:

Deuteronomy 30:19

[19] I call heaven and earth to record this day against you, *that* I have set before you **life** and death, **blessing** and cursing: therefore **choose life**, that both you and your seed may live.

Jesus came to give us life and life abundantly. He came to bless you and destroy the curse in your life. Let Heaven know you have chosen life and receive that life as your healing.

1 Kings 8:56

[56] Blessed *be* the LORD, which has given rest to His people Israel, according to all that He promised: **there has not failed one word of all His good promise**, which He promised by the hand of Moses His servant.

Did you grab this promise? There has not nor ever will fail any of His good promises. Store up these healing promises in your heart and believe that they will not fail you.

2 Kings 2:21-22

²¹ And he [Moses] went forth to the spring of the waters, and cast the salt in there, and said, Thus says the LORD, **I have healed these waters**; there shall **not be from here anymore death** or barren *land*. ²² So the waters were healed to this day, according to the saying of Elisha which he spake.

2 Kings 5:14

¹⁴ Then he [Naaman] went down, and dipped himself seven times in Jordan, according to the saying of the man of God: and his flesh came again like to the flesh of a little child, and **he was clean**.

1 Chronicles 29:28

²⁸ And he [David] **died in a good old age, full of days**, riches, and honor: and Solomon his son reigned in his stead.

2 Chronicles 30:20

²⁰ And the LORD hearkened to Hezekiah, and **healed** the people.

2 Kings 20:5

⁵ Thus says the LORD, the God of David your father, I have heard your [Hezekiah] prayer, I have seen your tears: behold, **I will heal you**: on the third day you shall go up to the house of the LORD.

Psalms 6:2
² Have mercy upon me, O LORD; for I *am* weak: O LORD, **heal me**; for my bones are vexed.

Ask in faith believing. God wants to heal you. You don't have to beg Him. He has already shown you His great mercy through Jesus. He has healed you already on the Cross. All you have to do is accept it. Receive it as yours.

Psalm 21:4
⁴ He asked life of you, *and* you gave *it* him, *even* **length of days** forever and ever.

Psalm 23:1-4
¹ The LORD *is* my shepherd; I shall not want. ² He makes me to lie down in green pastures: He leads me beside the still waters. ³ He restores my soul: He leads me in the paths of righteousness for His name's sake. ⁴ Yes, though I walk through the valley of the **shadow of death, I will fear no evil**: for **You** *are* **with me**; Your rod and Your staff they comfort me.

Death is but a shadow. Don't be afraid because Jesus is with you. He will never leave you nor forsake you. Walk through the valleys with praise and without fear.

Psalm 27:1
¹ The LORD *is* my light and my salvation; whom shall I fear? **The LORD** *is* **the strength of my life**; of whom shall I be afraid?

Psalm 28:7-8
⁷ The LORD *is* **my strength** and my shield; my heart trusted in Him, and **I am helped**: therefore my heart greatly rejoices;

and with my song will I praise Him. ⁸ The LORD *is* their strength, and He *is* the saving strength of his anointed.

Psalm 29:11
¹¹ The **LORD will give strength** to His people; the LORD will bless His people with **peace.**

Psalm 30:2
² O LORD my God, I cried to You, and You have **healed me**.

Psalm 34:19
¹⁹ **Many** *are* **the afflictions** of the righteous: but the LORD delivers him out of them **all.**

Psalm 42:11
¹¹ Why are you cast down, O my soul? and why are you disquieted within me? **Hope in God**: for I shall yet praise Him, *who is* **the health** of my countenance, and my God.

Psalm 67:2
² That Your way may be known upon earth, Your **saving health** among all nations.

Psalm 71:16
¹⁶ I will **go in the streng**th of the Lord GOD: I will make mention of Your righteousness, *even* of Yours only.

Psalm 73:26
²⁶ My flesh and my heart fail: *but* **God** *is* **the strength of my heart**, and my portion forever.

Psalm 84:5
⁵ Blessed *is* the man whose **strength *is* in You**; in whose heart *are* the ways *of them*.

Psalm 91:9-10
⁹ Because you have made the LORD, *which is* my refuge, *even* the most High, your habitation; ¹⁰ There shall no evil befall you, **neither shall any plague come near your dwelling.**

This is a promise to keep all those flu bugs away. Don't fear all the evil news of pandemic disease. No plague will come near you or your family.

Psalm 91:14-16
¹⁴ Because he has set his love upon Me, therefore will I deliver him: I will set him on high, because he has known My name. ¹⁵ He shall call upon Me, and I will answer him: **I *will be* with him in trouble**; I will deliver him, and honor him. ¹⁶ **With long life will I satisfy him**, and show him My salvation.

Here is another wonderful promise of long life. You don't have to leave until you are satisfied with life here.

Psalm 103:1-5
¹ Bless the LORD, O my soul: and all that is within me, *bless* His holy name. ² Bless the LORD, O my soul, and forget not all His benefits: ³ Who forgives all your iniquities; who **heals all your diseases**; ⁴ Who redeems your life from destruction; who crowns you with lovingkindness and tender mercies; ⁵ Who satisfies your mouth with good *things; so that* your **youth is renewed like the eagle's**.

Sickness is defeated, Amen

Psalm 105:37
³⁷ He brought them forth also with silver and gold: and *there was* **not one feeble** *person* among their tribes.

Psalm 107:19-21
¹⁹ Then they cry to the LORD in their trouble, *and* He saves them out of their distresses. ²⁰ **He sent His word, and healed them**, and delivered *them* from their destructions. ²¹ Oh that *men* would praise the LORD *for* His goodness, and *for* His wonderful works to the children of men!

Jesus is the Word. God sent the Word for your salvation and your healing. You are blessed.

Psalm 116:8
⁸ For You have **delivered my soul from death**, my eyes from tears, *and* my feet from falling.

Psalm 118:17
¹⁷ **I shall not die, but live**, and declare the works of the LORD.

Regardless of what you are facing, speak this word. Thank the Lord because His healing works. Thank Jesus for dying on the Cross that you can say "I shall not die."

Psalm 147:3
³ He **heals** the broken in heart, and binds up their wounds.

Proverbs 3:2
² For **length of days, and long life**, and **peace**, shall they add to you.

Here is a promise of peace through the tough times. No matter the situation, rest in the peace Jesus bought and provided for you.

Proverbs 3:7-8

[7] Be not wise in your own eyes: fear the LORD, and depart from evil. [8] It shall be **health** to your navel, and marrow to your bones.

Proverbs 4:20-23

[20] My son, attend to my words; incline your ear to my sayings. [21] Let them not depart from your eyes; keep them in the midst of your heart. [22] For they *are* **life** to those that find them, and **health** to all their flesh. [23] Keep your heart with all diligence; for out of it *are* the issues of life.

Keep the healing words of scripture remaining before your eyes. Get then deep down in your heart. The word is alive and powerful. The word is life and health. Hide them in your heart. Pull them out to remind yourself about the promises of God's healing for you.

Proverbs 9:11

[11] For by Me your **days shall be multiplied**, and the **years of your life shall be increased**.

Proverbs 12:18

[18] There is that [which] speaks like the piercings of a sword: but the tongue of the wise *is* **health.**

Speak health to yourself and others. Never speak death. Never use the word 'die' in a phrase, such as "I nearly died laughing." Only speak life. Speak health.

Proverbs 16:24

24 Pleasant words *are as* a honeycomb, sweet to the soul, and **health to the bones**.

Proverbs 17:22

22 A **merry heart does good *like* a medicine**: but a broken spirit dries the bones.

A joyful heart works wonders in the physical body. It acts like good medicine. Read the Word and rejoice in its promises for your healing. Stay happy. Be joy-filled no matter what.

Isaiah 40:29

29 He gives **power to the faint**; and to *them that have* no might **He increases strength**.

Isaiah 40:31

31 But they that wait upon the LORD shall **renew *their* strength**; they shall mount up with wings as eagles; **they shall run**, and not be weary; *and* **they shall walk**, and not faint.

The joy of the Lord is your strength. He will renew your strength. Wait in God's rest. Then get out there and walk in the strength of the Lord.

Isaiah 41:10

10 Fear not; for I *am* with you: be not dismayed; for I *am* your God: **I will strengthen you**; yes, I will help you; yes, I will uphold you with the right hand of My righteousness.

Isaiah 43:1-2

1 But now thus says the LORD that created you, O Jacob, and He that formed you, O Israel, Fear not: for I have redeemed you, I have called *you* by your name; you *are* mine. **² When you pass through the waters, I *will be* with you**; and through the rivers, they shall not overflow you: when you walk through the fire, you shall not be burned; neither shall the flame kindle upon you.

Isaiah 53:4-5
⁴ Surely **He has borne our griefs, and carried our sorrows**: yet we did esteem Him stricken, smitten of God, and afflicted. ⁵ But He *was* wounded for our transgressions, *He was* bruised for our iniquities: the chastisement of our peace *was* upon Him; and with **His stripes we are healed**.

Isaiah 57:18-19
¹⁸ I have seen his ways, and **will heal him**: I will lead him also, and **restore comforts** to him and to his mourners. ¹⁹ I create the fruit of the lips; Peace, peace to *him that is* far off, and to *him that is* near, says the LORD; **and I will heal him**.

Isaiah 58:8
⁸ Then shall your light break forth as the morning, and **your health shall spring forth speedily**: and your righteousness shall go before you; the glory of the LORD shall be your rear guard.

Isaiah 65:23
²³ They shall not labor in vain, nor bring forth for trouble; for they *are* **the seed of the blessed of the LORD**, and their offspring with them.

Jeremiah 1:12
¹² Then said the LORD to me, You have well seen: for **I will hasten My word to perform it.**

Jeremiah 17:14
¹⁴ **Heal me, O LORD, and I shall be healed**; save me, and I shall be saved: for you *are* my praise.

Jeremiah 30:17
¹⁷ For **I will restore health to thee**, and **I will heal you of your wounds**, says the LORD; because they called you an Outcast, *saying*, This *is* Zion, whom no man seeks after.

Jeremiah 33:6
⁶ Behold, **I will bring it health and cure**, and I will cure them, and will reveal to them the abundance of peace and truth.

Joel 3:10
¹⁰ ... **let the weak say, I *am* strong.**

Nahum 1:9
⁹ What do you imagine against the LORD? He will make **an utter end: affliction shall not rise up** the second time.

Malachi 4:2
² But to you that fear my name shall the Sun of righteousness arise with **healing in his wings**; and you shall go forth, and grow up as calves of the stall.

Chapter 2

Healing in the Gospels

Matthew 4:23-24
[23] And Jesus went about all Galilee, teaching in their synagogues, and preaching the gospel of the kingdom, and **healing all manner of sickness and all manner of disease** among the people. [24] And His fame went throughout all Syria: and they brought to Him **all sick people** that were taken with divers diseases and torments, and those who were possessed with devils, and those which were lunatic, and those that had the palsy; and **He healed them**.

Matthew 8:2-3
[2] And, behold, there came a leper and worshipped Him, saying, Lord, **if you will**, You can make me clean. [3] And Jesus put forth *His* hand, and touched him, saying, **I will; be clean.** And immediately his leprosy was cleansed.

Many people believe that God can heal, but they don't know if God will heal them. Jesus cleared that up when He said He was willing to heal. God wants to heal us. He isn't holding anything back and He isn't requiring something we can't do.

Matthew 8:5-13

⁵ And when Jesus was entered into Capernaum, there came to Him a centurion, beseeching Him, ⁶ And saying, Lord, my servant lies at home sick of the palsy, grievously tormented. ⁷ And Jesus said to him, **I will come and heal him**. ⁸ The centurion answered and said, Lord, I am not worthy that You should come under my roof: but speak the word only, and my servant shall be healed. ⁹ For I am a man under authority, having soldiers under me: and I say to this *man*, Go, and he goes; and to another, Come, and he comes; and to my servant, Do this, and he does *it*. ¹⁰ When Jesus heard *it*, He marveled, and said to them that followed, Verily I say to you, I have not found so great faith, no, not in Israel. ¹¹ And I say to you, That many shall come from the east and west, and shall sit down with Abraham, and Isaac, and Jacob, in the kingdom of heaven. ¹² But the children of the kingdom shall be cast out into outer darkness: there shall be weeping and gnashing of teeth. ¹³ And Jesus said to the centurion, Go your way; and as you have believed, *so* be it done to you. And **his servant was healed** in the selfsame hour.

This passage answers many questions but notice Jesus totally ignored the centurion's words about him not being worthy. We are all unworthy. Jesus doesn't heal because we are somehow worthy to be healed. Jesus heals because He loves. We are healed through Jesus who is the only one worthy. He doesn't want His children sick.

Matthew 8:14-15

14 And when Jesus was come into Peter's house, He saw his wife's mother laid, and **sick of a fever**. **15** And He touched her hand, and **the fever left** her: and she arose, and ministered to them.

Matthew 8:16-17

16 When the evening was come, they brought to Him many that were possessed with devils: and He cast out the spirits with *His* word, and **healed all that were sick**: **17** That it might be fulfilled which was spoken by Isaiah the prophet, saying, **Himself took our infirmities, and bare *our* sicknesses.**

Matthew 8:19-20

19 Again I say unto you, That if two of you shall agree on earth as touching anything that they shall ask, **it shall be done for them** of my Father which is in heaven. **20** For where two or three are gathered together in my name, there am I in the midst of them.

Find a trusted prayer partner who believes as you do. This is a person you can agree with and one who can agree with you. Putting your name on the "prayer chain" is okay, but healing doesn't come by the number of people you have praying. Some prayer chains are just notifications that you are sick. Sometimes people will tell others that they are believing for their healing. They think that the more people they tell, that God will have to do something because He won't want to embarrass you if you don't get healed. That's trying to manipulate God and it won't work. Jesus says it only takes two to agree on anything and the Father will answer.

Matthew 9:20-21

20 And, behold, a woman, who was diseased with an issue of blood twelve years, came behind *Him*, and touched the hem of His garment: **21** For she said within herself, If I may but touch His garment, **I shall be whole**.

This woman believed for her healing. We don't know how many times she said, "If I but touch His garment, I shall be whole." But she believed it. She did whatever was needed to touch His garment. She was made whole, completely free of and sickness through the miracle working power of Jesus.

Matthew 9:23-26

23 And when Jesus came into the ruler's house, and saw the minstrels and the people making a noise, **24** He said to them, give place: for **the maid is not dead**, but sleeps. And they laughed Him to scorn. **25** But when the people were put forth, He went in, and took her by the hand, and the maid arose. **26** And the fame hereof went abroad into all that land.

Matthew 9:27-31

27 And when Jesus departed from there, two blind men followed Him, crying, and saying, *You* Son of David, have mercy on us. **28** And when He was come into the house, the blind men came to him: and Jesus said to them, **Do you believe that I am able to do this?** They said to Him, Yes, Lord. **29** Then He touched their eyes, saying, **According to your faith** be it to you. **30** And their eyes were opened; and Jesus sternly charged them, saying, See *that* no man know *it*. **31** But they, when they were departed, spread abroad his fame in all that country.

Matthew 9:35

35 And Jesus went about all the cities and villages, teaching in their synagogues, and preaching the gospel of the kingdom, and **healing every sickness and every disease** among the people.

Jesus went through all the cities teaching, preaching, and healing. He healed every sickness and disease. There were no diseases that were too hard for Him to heal. He healed the smallest sickness to the most severe. He healed every one of every disease.

Matthew 10:1

¹ And when He had called to *Him* His twelve disciples, He gave them power *against* unclean spirits, to cast them out, and **to heal all manner of sickness and all manner of disease.**

Jesus sent His disciples out to heal all manner of sickness and disease. It didn't matter the problem, they were called to heal it all. And Jesus wasn't with them in person.

Matthew 10:8

⁸ **Heal the sick**, cleanse the lepers, raise the dead, cast out devils: **freely** you have received, freely give.

Your healing is a free gift. That's grace. Freely given to you. It's yours.

Matthew 11:4-5

⁴ Jesus answered and said to them, Go and show John [the Baptist] again those things which you do hear and see: ⁵ The blind receive their sight, and the lame walk, the lepers are cleansed, and the deaf hear, the dead are raised up, and the poor have the gospel preached to them.

Matthew 11:28-30

²⁸ Come to me, all *you* that labor and are heavy laden, and **I will give you rest**. ²⁹ Take My yoke upon you, and learn of

me; for I am meek and lowly in heart: and you shall find rest for your souls. **30** For my yoke *is* easy, and my burden is light.

Matthew 12:10-13

10 And, behold, there was a man who had *his* hand withered. And they asked Him, saying, Is it lawful to heal on the sabbath days? that they might accuse Him. **11** And He said to them, What man shall there be among you, that shall have one sheep, and if it fall into a pit on the sabbath day, will he not lay hold on it, and lift *it* out? **12** How much then is a man better than a sheep? Wherefore it is lawful to do well on the sabbath days. **13** Then He said to the man, Stretch forth your hand. And he stretched *it* forth; and **it was restored whole**, like as the other.

The scribes and Pharisees were all the time trying to use the law to keep Jesus from healing on the Sabbath. Jesus, who never disobeyed the law, showed them that they twisted the law for their uses and that God never meant for the law to challenge healing. Love is the fulfillment of the law.

Matthew 12:15

15 But when Jesus knew *it*, He withdrew Himself from there: and great multitudes followed Him, and **He healed them all**.

Notice how many times scripture says that Jesus healed them all. They weren't "saved" nor was their behavior perfect. There is no one that Jesus didn't heal. He healed them all and that includes you.

Matthew 12:22

22 Then was brought to Him one possessed with a devil, blind, and dumb: and He **healed him**, insomuch that the blind and dumb both spoke and saw.

Matthew 13:15-16

¹⁵ For this people's heart is waxed gross, and *their* ears are dull of hearing, and their eyes they have closed; lest at any time they should see with *their* eyes, and hear with *their* ears, and should understand with *their* heart, and should be converted, and I should **heal them**. ¹⁶ But blessed *are* your eyes, for they see: and your ears, for they hear.

People aren't healed because they don't know Jesus heals. They don't understand the finished of Jesus on the Cross. He is the Word that the Father sent to bring healing.

Matthew 14:13-14

¹³ When Jesus heard *of it*, He departed there by ship into a desert place apart: and when the people had heard *thereof*, they followed Him on foot out of the cities. ¹⁴ And Jesus went forth, and saw a great multitude, and was moved with compassion toward them, and **He healed their sick**.

Even though Jesus as a man needed to get away to rest and renew His spirit with the Father, He put that aside because of His great compassion and healed all the sick people that came to Him.

Matthew 14:34-36

³⁴ And when they were gone over, they came into the land of Gennesaret. ³⁵ And when the men of that place had knowledge of Him, they sent out into all that country round about, and brought to Him all that were **diseased**; ³⁶ And besought Him that they might only touch the hem of His garment: and as many as touched were **made perfectly whole.**

During the time Jesus was physically on the earth, people who even touched the edge of His garment were healed. We can't physically touch Him but we touch Him by faith. We know Jesus dwells in us now but sometimes it helps to just see yourself reaching out and touching Jesus.

Matthew 15:28

28 Then Jesus answered and said to her, O woman, great *is* your faith: be it to you even as you will. And her daughter **was made whole** from that very hour.

Matthew 15:30-31

30 And **great multitudes came to Him**, having with them *those that were* lame, blind, dumb, maimed, and many others, and cast them down at Jesus' feet; **and He healed them**: **31** Insomuch that the multitude wondered, when they saw the dumb to speak, the maimed to be whole, the lame to walk, and the blind to see: and they glorified the God of Israel.

Matthew 18:18-19

18 Verily I say to you, whatever you bind on earth shall be bound in heaven: and whatever you loose on earth shall be loosed in heaven. **19** Again I say to you, that if two of you shall agree on earth as touching anything that they shall ask, **it shall be done** for them of my Father who is in heaven.

Have a prayer partner praying for you who is in complete agreement with you for your complete healing. Use this promise as yours when you agree with another person.

Matthew 19:2

2 And great multitudes followed Him; and He **healed them** there.

Matthew 21:14

14 And the blind and the lame came to Him in the temple; and **He healed** them.

Matthew 21:21-22

²¹ Jesus answered and said to them, Verily I say to you, If you have faith, and doubt not, you shall not only do this *which is done* to the fig tree [the previous day He had cursed the fig tree and it dried up], but also if **you shall say** to this mountain, Be removed, and be cast into the sea; it shall be done. ²² And all things, whatever you shall ask in prayer, believing, you shall receive.

Your sickness and ill health is a mountain. Speak to the mountain out loud to be removed. Jesus said it will be done for you as you exercise your faith. Don't doubt that God wants to heal you.

Mark 1:29-34

²⁹ And immediately, when they were come out of the synagogue, they entered into the house of Simon and Andrew, with James and John. ³⁰ But Simon's wife's mother lay sick of a fever, and immediately they tell Him of her. ³¹ And He came and took her by the hand, and lifted her up; and **immediately the fever left her**, and she ministered to them. ³² And at even, when the sun did set, they brought to Him all that were diseased, and them that were possessed with devils. ³³ And all the city was gathered together at the door. ³⁴ And **He healed** many that were sick of divers diseases, and cast out many devils; and suffered not the devils to speak, because they knew Him.

Mark 1:40-41

⁴⁰ And there came a leper to Him, beseeching him, and kneeling down to Him, and saying to Him, If You will, You can make me clean. ⁴¹ And Jesus, moved with compassion, **put forth *His* hand, and touched him**, and said to him, I will; be clean.

Jesus was not afraid to touch the leper. Though lepers were not to be around people and hadn't been touched by anyone in a long time, Jesus reached out and touched the leper and he was made whole. Jesus is greater than any illness or disease.

Mark 2:11-12

¹¹ I say to you, Arise, and take up your bed, and go your way into your house. ¹² And immediately he arose, took up the bed, and went forth before them all; insomuch that they were all amazed, and glorified God, saying, We never saw it on this fashion.

They glorified and praised God when they saw the miracles Jesus did. We see the miracle by faith and we glorify and praise God even before we see the complete manifestation of our healing.

Mark 3:1-5

¹ And He entered again into the synagogue; and there was a man there who had a withered hand. ² And they watched Him, whether He would heal him on the Sabbath day; that they might accuse Him. ³ And He said to the man who had the withered hand, Stand forth. ⁴ And He said to them, Is it lawful to do good on the sabbath days, or to do evil? To save life, or to kill? But they held their peace. ⁵ And when He had looked round about on them with anger, being grieved for the hardness of their hearts, He said to the man, Stretch forth your hand. And he stretched *it* out: and his hand was restored whole as the other.

This is the only time it is recorded that Jesus was angry. He was angry at people who tried to keep the man from getting healed. He was angry at sickness and disease that tried to hurt the people. He was grieved because the people were so concerned about their wrong interpretation of the law that they failed to have compassion on the hurting person. God wants you well.

Mark 3:10
10 For He had **healed many**; insomuch that they pressed upon Him for to touch Him, as many as had plagues.

Mark 3:15
15 And to have **power to heal sicknesses**, and to cast out devils:

Mark 9:23
23 Jesus said to him, If you can believe, all things *are* possible to him that believes.

Mark 6:5-6
5 And He could there do no mighty work, save that He laid His hands upon a few sick folk, and **healed** *them*. **6** And He marveled because of their unbelief. And He went round about the villages, teaching.

He couldn't heal there because the power of unbelief was preventing the healing to flow. Don't let anyone steal your healing through their unbelief. You just trust the Lord for your healing and don't listen to the naysayers.

Mark 6:13
13 And they cast out many devils, and anointed with oil many that were sick, and healed *them*.

This is the only place in the gospels where it said they used oil to anoint the sick for healing. Anointing oil was commonly used in the Old Testament. We will see in James that the church will use it also. Oil doesn't heal, Jesus heals. Sometimes oil acts as a point of faith and helps release the faith to heal and dispels the doubts. See James 5:14.

Mark 6:55-56

⁵⁵ And [the people seeing Jesus get off the boat] ran through that whole region round about, and began to carry about in beds those that were sick, where they heard He was. ⁵⁶ And wherever He entered, into villages, or cities, or country, they laid the sick in the streets, and besought Him that they might touch if it were but the border of His garment: and as many as touched Him **were made whole**.

Mark 7:25-30

²⁵ For a *certain* woman, whose young daughter had an unclean spirit, heard of Him, and came and fell at His feet: ²⁶ The woman was a Greek, a Syrophenician by nation; and she besought Him that He would cast forth the devil out of her daughter. ²⁷ But Jesus said to her, Let the children first be filled: for it is not meet to take the children's bread, and to cast *it* to the dogs. ²⁸ And she answered and said to him, Yes, Lord: yet the dogs under the table eat of the children's crumbs. ²⁹ And He said to her, for this saying go your way; the devil is gone out of your daughter. ³⁰ And when she was come to her house, she **found the devil gone** out, and her daughter laid upon the bed.

Jesus is not respecter of persons. Here a Greek woman came to Jesus for her daughter's healing. He tested her by basically telling her that He had not come to the Gentiles but to Israel. He sounded rather harsh calling her a dog. Jesus who was under the law, had to show the separation of Israel from other nations under the law. Had she taken offence, she would not have gotten her desire. But she persisted. She took a step of faith believing even a crumb from Jesus was enough to heal her daughter. Though she wasn't a child of Israel, she still saw in Jesus the compassion of the healer. Since the Cross, however, there is no separation. Everyone can choose to be a child of God and can come to Jesus for their healing.

Mark 7:31-37

31 And again, departing from the coasts of Tyre and Sidon, He came to the sea of Galilee, through the midst of the coasts of Decapolis. **32** And they brought to Him one that was deaf, and had an impediment in his speech; and they beseech Him to put His hand upon him. **33** And He took him aside from the multitude, and put His fingers into his ears, and He spit, and touched his tongue; **34** And looking up to heaven, He sighed, and said to him, Ephphatha, that is, Be opened. **35** And straightway **his ears were opened**, and the string of his **tongue was loosed**, and he spoke plain. **36** And He charged them that they should tell no man: but the more He charged them, so much the more a great deal they published *it*; **37** and were beyond measure astonished, saying, He has done all things well: He makes both the deaf to hear, and the dumb to speak.

A couple of times Mark records that Jesus used His spit in the course of healing. In the case of Jesus, even His spit had power to heal. Unfortunately, we sometimes take what Jesus did and make it a healing procedure. Jesus didn't mean for us to start healing by spitting on people. Jesus would spit on some for good, healing them. Yet He was spat upon for evil by those who didn't know Him. Jesus is the healer and we look to Him by faith. He has conquered sickness and disease for our healing.

Mark 8:22-25

22 And He comes to Bethsaida; and they bring a blind man to Him, and besought Him to touch him. **23** And He took the blind man by the hand, and led him out of the town; and when He had spit on his eyes, and put His hands upon him, He asked him if he saw ought. **24** And he looked up, and said, I see men as trees, walking. **25** After that He put *His* hands again upon his eyes, and made him look up: and **he was restored**, and saw every man clearly.

When I see this passage, I see that Jesus had to take the blind man away from the unbelief prevalent in the town. It also shows that sometimes healing doesn't happen instantly. Healing may come a little at a time, but it still comes; and the end result is total wellness.

Mark 9:17-25

¹⁷ And one of the multitude answered and said, Master, I have brought to You my son, who has a dumb spirit; ¹⁸ And wherever he takes him, he tears him: and he foams, and gnashes with his teeth, and pines away: and I spoke to your disciples that they should cast him out; and they could not. ¹⁹ He answered him, and said, O faithless generation, how long shall I be with you? How long shall I suffer you? Bring him to Me. ²⁰ And they brought him to Him: and when he saw Him, straightway the spirit tore him; and he fell on the ground, and wallowed foaming. ²¹ And He asked his father, how long is it ago since this came to him? And he said, Of a child. ²² And oftentimes it has cast him into the fire, and into the waters, to destroy him: but if You can do anything, have compassion on us, and help us. ²³ Jesus said to him, If you can believe, all things *are* possible to him that believes. ²⁴ And straightway the father of the child cried out, and said with tears, **Lord, I believe; help my unbelief**. ²⁵ When Jesus saw that the people came running together, He rebuked the foul spirit, saying to him, *You* dumb and deaf spirit, I charge you, come out of him, and enter no more into him.

Two things we face when we pray—believing in faith or unbelief. Sometime we can ask in faith but doubts and unbelief creep in. The father in this passage recognized the problem. We can believe for what seems impossible, but we need help for the unbelief that says we really don't expect it to happen to us. Jesus will help with your unbelief. Just see Him healing. Imagine Him healing you. When the symptoms persist, just continue to believe for the impossible and ask Jesus to help you release all doubts to the fact He will heal you.

Mark 10:27

27 And Jesus looking upon them said, With men *it is* impossible, but not with God: for with God all things are possible.

Just put this deep down into your heart. Nothing is impossible for God. Whether it's a cold or a serious illness makes no difference to God's ability to heal. What's impossible for man is possible with God.

Mark 11:22-24

22 And Jesus answering said to them, Have faith in God. **23** For verily I say to you, That whoever shall say to this mountain, Be removed, and be cast into the sea; and shall not doubt in his heart, but shall believe that those things which he says shall come to pass; he shall have whatever he says. **24** Therefore I say to you, What things soever you desire, when you pray, believe that you receive *them*, and you shall have *them*.

This is the zenith of faith God wants us to have all wrapped up in three verses. First, speak to the mountain. Don't speak to God about your mountain. Speak to your mountain about your God. Second, speak whatever it is you desire. Then ask God believing that Jesus has already done everything on the Cross to insure your healing. Believe that healing is part of that finished work and believe that when you ask, you have what you asked for. See Jesus pulling your healing off the shelf and shipping it to you. See yourself receiving that gift. Don't let doubt creep in. Take it. Just believe that no matter what, you will be healed.

Mark 16:14-18

14 Afterward He appeared to the eleven as they sat at meat, and upbraided them with their unbelief and hardness of heart, because they believed not them who had seen Him after He was risen. **15** And He said to them, Go you into all the world, and preach the gospel to every creature. **16** He that believes and is baptized shall be saved; but he that believes not shall be damned. ⁱ⁷ And these signs shall follow them that believe; In my name shall they cast out devils; they shall speak with new tongues; ¹⁸ They shall take up serpents; and if they drink any deadly thing, it shall not hurt them; **they shall lay hands on the sick, and they shall recover**.

Healing didn't stop with Jesus. He charged His disciples to do the same as He had done. Preach the gospel of good news and go about healing the sick. This is a charge to all disciples, and those who would ever become disciples, not just those in His hearing that day. Just as the charge to preach went out and has continued to today, so does the charge to lay hands on the sick and they shall recover.

Luke 4:18

¹⁸ The Spirit of the Lord *is* upon Me, because He has anointed Me to preach the gospel to the poor; He has sent Me **to heal** the brokenhearted, to **preach deliverance** to the captives, and **recovering** of sight to the blind, to **set at liberty** them that are bruised.

Luke 4:38-40

³⁸ And He arose out of the synagogue, and entered into Simon's house. And Simon's wife's mother was taken with a great fever; and they besought Him for her. ³⁹ And He stood over her, and **rebuked the fever**; and it left her: and immediately she arose and ministered to them. ⁴⁰ Now when the sun was setting, all they that had any sick with divers diseases brought them to Him; and **He laid His hands on every one of them, and healed them.**

Luke 5:13-15

¹³ And He put forth *His* hand, and touched him [leper who came to Jesus], saying, I will: **be clean**. And immediately the leprosy departed from him. ¹⁴ And He charged him to tell no

man: but go, and show yourself to the priest, and offer for your cleansing, according as Moses commanded, for a testimony to them. ¹⁵ But so much the more went there a fame abroad of Him: and great multitudes came together to hear, and to be healed by Him of their infirmities.

Luke 5:17-26

¹⁷ And it came to pass on a certain day, as He was teaching, that there were Pharisees and doctors of the law sitting by, who were come out of every town of Galilee, and Judea, and Jerusalem: and **the power of the Lord was *present* to heal them**. ¹⁸ And, behold, men brought in a bed a man who was taken with a palsy: and they sought *means* to bring him in, and to lay *him* before Him. ¹⁹ And when they could not find by what *way* they might bring him in because of the multitude, they went upon the housetop, and let him down through the tiling with *his* couch into the midst before Jesus. ²⁰ And when He saw their faith, He said to him, Man, your sins are forgiven you. ²¹ And the scribes and the Pharisees began to reason, saying, Who is this who speaks blasphemies? Who can forgive sins, but God alone? ²² But when Jesus perceived their thoughts, He answering said to them, Why reason you in your hearts? ²³ Whether is easier, to say, you sins be forgiven you; or to say, Rise up and walk? ²⁴ But that you may know that the Son of man has power upon earth to forgive sins, (He said to the sick of the palsy,) I say to you, Arise, and take up your couch, and go into your house. ²⁵ And **immediately he rose up** before them, and took up that whereon he lay, and departed to his own house, glorifying God. ²⁶ And they were all amazed, and they glorified God, and were filled with fear, saying, **We have seen strange things to day.**

Jesus first forgave the man of his sins. It's hard to receive from Jesus if you think your sins are preventing you from receiving. God wanted him to know that He was not holding his sins against him—that what he had done in the past was forgiven and was just that, in the past. The same is true for us today. Jesus went to the Cross so that all our sins could be forgiven—past, present and future. God remembers your sins no more. So your sins are not preventing you from being healed. God loves you and wants you well. When God looks at you, He sees what Jesus has done for you. You are free from the dominion of sin and your sins are no longer holding you ransom. You are holy and perfect in His eyes.

Luke 6:6-10

⁶ And it came to pass also on another Sabbath that He entered into the synagogue and taught: and there was a man whose right hand was withered. ⁷ And the scribes and Pharisees watched him, whether He would heal on the Sabbath day; that they might find an accusation against Him. ⁸ But He knew their thoughts, and said to the man who had the withered hand, Rise up, and stand forth in the midst. And he arose and stood forth. ⁹ Then Jesus said to them, I will ask you one thing; Is it lawful on the sabbath days to do good, or to do evil? to save life, or to destroy *it*? ¹⁰ And looking round about upon them all, He said to the man, Stretch forth your hand. And he did so: and **his hand was restored** whole as the other.

Ask yourself, does God want to do you evil or good? Does He want to Heal you or destroy you? The answer is obvious since Jesus went on to heal. If it's good, it comes from God. If it's bad (your sickness), it didn't come from Him. Never think that God wants you sick to teach you something. Jesus made it clear that He wants you well. If you need to learn something, that's why God gave us the Word.

Luke 6:17-18

¹⁷ And He came down with them, and stood in the plain, and the company of His disciples, and a great multitude of

people out of all Judea and Jerusalem, and from the sea coast of Tyre and Sidon, who came to hear Him, and to be healed of their diseases; **18** And they that were vexed with unclean spirits: and *they were healed*.

The problem of evil spirits overly concerns believers. In this passage, it says they were vexed by unclean spirits. In other words they harassed, tormented, troubled and oppressed by evil spirits. In other places, it says that Jesus cast out demons, as they inhabited people. Jesus came to destroy the works of the devil (1 John 3:18). Demons cannot dwell in believers. God isn't sharing His temple with the devil. But the devil will still try to harass you with symptoms and trouble you with doubts about promises of your healing. But you don't have to accept anything with which the devil tries to trouble you. You are free from the snares of the devil. You have the armor on and are standing against a toothless roaring lion. Don't be concerned about the source of your sickness. It's all from the devil anyway. Simply look to Jesus who has already defeated the devil on your behalf. Accept your healing and don't allow the enemy to steal it from you.

Luke 6:19

19 And the whole multitude sought to touch Him: for there went virtue out of Him, and **healed *them* all**.

Virtue here is not just His goodness, but the word is the Greek for dynamite power. Miracle healing power flowed from Jesus. He is still the same today. Appropriate His mighty dynamite healing power.

Luke 7:2-10

2 And a certain centurion's servant, who was dear to him, was sick, and ready to die. **3** And when he heard of Jesus, he sent to Him the elders of the Jews, beseeching Him that He would come and heal his servant. **4** And when they came to Jesus, they besought Him instantly, saying, That he was worthy for whom He should do this: **5** For he loves our nation, and he has built us a synagogue. **6** Then Jesus went with them. And when He was now not far from the house, the centurion sent friends to him, saying to him, Lord, trouble not thyself: for I am not worthy that You should enter under my roof: **7** Wherefore neither thought I myself worthy to come to You: but say in a word, and my servant shall be healed. **8** For I also am a man set under authority, having under me soldiers, and I say to one, Go, and he goes; and to another, Come, and he comes; and to my servant, Do this, and he does *it*. **9** When Jesus heard these things, He marveled at him, and turned Him about, and said to the people that followed Him, I say to you, I have not found so great faith, no, not in Israel. **10** And they that were sent, returning to the house, found the **servant whole that had been sick.**

As so often happened in the ministry of Jesus, the non-Jew showed more faith than His own people. Here a Roman caused Jesus to marvel at his faith, faith He hadn't seen in Israel. Jesus didn't go to the centurion's house because he was worthy, even though they tried to persuade Jesus that he was. Even the centurion didn't consider himself worthy. But Jesus dismissed it all. He marveled at his faith—the centurion knew that Jesus had only to speak a word and his servant would be healed. That's the amazing faith that Jesus saw and why his servant was healed. So you don't come to Jesus for your healing based on any self-worth or lack of it. It's all based on grace through faith. Jesus has done all the work.

Luke 7:12-15

12 Now when He came near to the gate of the city, behold, there was a dead man carried out, the only son of his mother, and she was a widow: and much people of the city was with her. **13** And when the Lord saw her, He had compassion on her, and said to her, Weep not. **14** And He came and touched the bier: and they that bare *him* stood still. And He said, Young man, I say to your, Arise. **15** And he that was dead sat up, and began to speak. And He delivered him to his mother.

Here is an example of Jesus raising the dead. Several Gospel accounts record Jesus doing that. It just shows that death has no power over Him or better, that He had power over death. Death is an enemy. Though we all have to die, unless the Lord returns, Jesus displayed that sometimes it's not the right time. Jesus had compassion on the widow who would have been left alone without her son to help her. Jesus delivered him back to his mother. Jesus has the power over death.

Luke 7:22

22 Then Jesus answering said to them, Go your way, and tell John [the Baptist] what things you have seen and heard; how that the **blind see**, the **lame walk**, the **lepers are cleansed**, the **deaf hear**, the **dead are raised**, to the poor the gospel is preached.

Luke 8:2

2 And certain women, who had been **healed of evil spirits and infirmities**, Mary called Magdalene, out of whom went seven devils.

Luke 8:36

36 They also which saw *it* told them by what means he that was possessed of the devils **was healed**.

Luke 8:43-48

43 And a woman having an issue of blood twelve years, who had spent all her living upon physicians, neither could be healed of any, 44 Came behind *Him*, and touched the border of His garment: and immediately her issue of blood stopped. 45 And Jesus said, who touched Me? When all denied, Peter and they that were with Him said, Master, the multitude throng You and press *You*, and say You, Who touched Me? 46 And Jesus said, somebody has touched Me: for I perceive

that virtue [miracle working power] is gone out of Me. ⁴⁷ And when the woman saw that she was not hid, she came trembling, and falling down before him, she declared to Him before all the people for what cause she had touched Him, and how **she was healed** immediately. ⁴⁸ And He said to her, Daughter, be of good comfort: **Your faith has made you whole**; go in peace.

Here is an example of a woman who had been having physical problems for many years. She did what she knew to do. Doctors today know much more about helping heal the body. It's not wrong to go to a doctor. I believe any knowledge they have comes from God anyway. See Appendix A for more about going to a doctor. When doctors couldn't help, this woman heard about Jesus. Jesus fame was renown throughout Israel for His healing power. So this woman simply believed that when she just touched His garment she would be healed. And she was. She stepped out by faith knowing she was violating religious laws but desiring her healing more than the consequences of her actions. She broke her way through the crowd and against all obstacles made her way to Jesus. The miracle working power of Jesus flowed into her and she was immediately healed. Jesus called that faith to be made whole. Don't let any obstacle keep you from that same faith for your healing. Touch the hem and be healed.

Luke 8:41-42, 49-56

⁴¹ And behold, there came a man named Jairus, and he was a ruler of the synagogue. And he fell down at Jesus' feet and begged Him to come to his house, ⁴² for he had an only daughter about twelve years of age, and she was dying. But as He went, the multitudes thronged Him.... ⁴⁹ While He yet spoke, there comes one from the ruler of the synagogue's *house*, saying to Him, Your daughter is dead; trouble not the Master. ⁵⁰ But when Jesus heard *it*, He answered him, saying, **Fear not: believe only**, and she shall be made whole. ⁵¹ And when He came into the house, He suffered no man to go in, except Peter, and James, and John, and the

father and the mother of the maiden. ⁵² And all wept, and bewailed her: but He said, Weep not; she is not dead, but sleeps. ⁵³ And they laughed Him to scorn, knowing that she was dead. ⁵⁴ And He put them all out, and took her by the hand, and called, saying, Maid, arise. ⁵⁵ And her spirit came again, and **she arose straightway**: and He commanded to give her meat. ⁵⁶ And her parents were astonished: but He charged them that they should tell no man what was done.

When things looked their worse, Jesus just told them not to fear (fear not), just keep believing. At the first sign of problems we tend to react in fear. Fear kills belief. Jesus simply said – don't fear. When signs of trouble or complications arise, don't fear. Don't anticipate the worse, but believe for the best. Perfect love drives out fear. Allow the perfect love of God for you drive out any fear. Keep praising God for His healing.

Luke 9:1-2

¹ Then He called His twelve disciples together, and gave them power and authority over all devils, and **to cure diseases**. ² And He sent them to preach the kingdom of God, and **to heal the sick**.

Notice the two things Jesus wanted His disciples to do. First, preach the good news of the kingdom of God. They couldn't yet preach the gospel of the Cross, but they preached that the kingdom of God was very near them; and second, that Jesus wanted them to heal the sick. Healing was both a proof that the Kingdom of God was there, but also because Jesus had such compassion for the sick. Sickness was a sign that not all was well. Jesus came making people well—a sure sign that the King of the Kingdom of God was there.

Luke 9:6

⁶ And they departed, and went through the towns, preaching the gospel, and **healing everywhere.**

Luke 9:11

¹¹ And the people, when they knew *it*, followed Him: and He received them, and spoke to them of the kingdom of God, and **healed them that had need of healing**.

Luke 9:38-39, 42

³⁸ Suddenly a man from the multitude cried out, saying, "Teacher, I implore You, look on my son, for he is my only child. ³⁹ And behold, a spirit seizes him, and he suddenly cries out; it convulses him so that he foams *at the mouth*, and it departs from him with great difficulty, bruising him…. ⁴² And as he was yet coming, the devil threw him down, and tore *him*. And Jesus rebuked the unclean spirit, and **healed the child**, and delivered him again to his father.

Luke 9:56

⁵⁶ For the Son of man is not come to destroy men's lives, but **to save** *them*. And they went to another village.

Jesus came to save—sozo. This word means to rescue, save, heal, make whole, restore, and free. God wants you saved physically and eternally. Jesus came to save, not to destroy. God wants you well, not sick. He always wants your best. He's the ultimate good Father.

Luke 10:9

⁹ And **heal the sick** that are therein, and say to them, the kingdom of God is come near to you.

Luke 13:16

¹⁶ And ought not this woman, being a daughter of Abraham, whom Satan has bound, lo, these eighteen years, be loosed from this bond on the sabbath day?

Here's another example of how Satan deceives people. He had this woman bound to her illness for 18 years. Jesus loosed her from this bondage. Jesus went to the Cross to free us from the bondage of sin and death. You are free from the bondage of Satan. Take your freedom in faith by trusting Jesus for total freedom from your illness.

Luke 14:3-4

³ And Jesus answering spoke to the lawyers and Pharisees, saying, Is it lawful to heal on the Sabbath day? ⁴ And they held their peace. And He took *him*, **and healed him**, and let him go.

Luke 17:14-15

¹⁴ And when He saw *them* [10 lepers asking for Jesus to heal them], He said to them, Go show yourselves to the priests. And it came to pass, that, as they went, they were cleansed. ¹⁵ And one of them, when he saw that he **was healed**, turned back, and with a loud voice glorified God.

Don't take your healing for granted. Glorify God for your healing. Thank Him and be a testimony to His healing power.

Luke 18:42-43

⁴² And Jesus said to him, **Receive your sight: your faith has saved you**. ⁴³ And immediately he received his sight, and followed Him, glorifying God: and all the people, when they saw *it*, gave praise to God.

Luke 22:19-20

¹⁹ And He took bread, and gave thanks, and broke *it*, and gave to them, saying, This is My body which is given for you: this do in remembrance of Me. ²⁰ Likewise also the cup after

supper, saying, This cup *is* the New Testament in my blood, which is shed for you.

Taking communion is a good way to receive your healing. See Appendix B for additional notes.

Luke 22:50-51

⁵⁰ And one of them struck the servant of the high priest, and cut off his right ear. ⁵¹ And Jesus answered and said, Suffer you thus far. And He touched his ear, and **healed him**.

John 4:46-53

⁴⁶ And there was a certain nobleman, whose son was sick at Capernaum. ⁴⁷ When he heard that Jesus was come out of Judea into Galilee, he went to Him, and besought Him that He would come down, and heal his son: for he was at the point of death. ⁴⁸ Then Jesus said to him, Except you see signs and wonders, you will not believe. ⁴⁹ The nobleman said to him, Sir, come down or my child die. ⁵⁰ Jesus said to him, Go your way; **your son lives**. And **the man believed the word that Jesus had spoken** to him, and he went his way. ⁵¹ And as he was now going down, his servants met him, and told *him*, saying, your son lives. ⁵² Then he enquired of them the hour when he began to amend. And they said to him, Yesterday at the seventh hour **the fever left** him. ⁵³ So the father knew that *it was* at the same hour, in which Jesus said to him, your son lives: and himself believed, and his whole house.

This nobleman believed the word that Jesus had spoken. We don't physically hear Jesus speak, but we have His word. He is the Word of God. His words are eternal. His words work now 2000 years after He spoke them just as if He had said them directly to us. This is why you are reading the Word. You are hearing what Jesus has said and you are believing the Word Jesus has spoken.

John 5:2-13

2 Now there is at Jerusalem by the sheep *market* a pool, which is called in the Hebrew tongue Bethesda, having five porches. **3** In these lay a great multitude of impotent folk, of blind, halt, withered, waiting for the moving of the water. **4** For an angel went down at a certain season into the pool, and troubled the water: whoever then first after the troubling of the water stepped in **was made whole of whatever disease he had**. **5** And a certain man was there, who had an infirmity thirty and eight years. **6** When Jesus saw him lie, and knew that he had been now a long time *in that case*, He said to him, Will you be made whole? **7** The impotent man answered Him, Sir, I have no man, when the water is troubled, to put me into the pool: but while I am coming, another steps down before me. **8** Jesus said to him, Rise, take up your bed, and walk. **9** And immediately the man **was made whole**, and took up his bed, and walked: and on the same day was the Sabbath. **10** The Jews therefore said to him that was cured, It is the sabbath day: it is not lawful for you to carry *your* bed. **11** He answered them, He that made me whole, the same said to me, Take up your bed, and walk. **12** Then asked they him, What man is that who said to you, Take up your bed, and walk? **13** And he that was healed knew not who it was: for Jesus had conveyed Himself away, a multitude being in *that* place.

*We live in a society where we try to explain things through science or experience or even speculation. Many have tried to explain in the natural that this pond had medicinal qualities that bubbled up at a certain time and the first one in was healed and the bubbling subsided. But have you ever heard of a medicinal pond that could cure "**whatever disease he had?** Jesus said nothing about the water. He chose one man to heal there. I think we need to understand this passage just as it says it. Bethesda means house of mercy. God had mercy on the people there and sent an angel occasionally to stir up the water so the people could step in and be healed. It wasn't the water. It wasn't the angel. It was God* *who healed. Certainly the first one in the water actually was healed. They all knew it and this man had been coming a long time. The important thing is that Jesus stepped in at that moment and healed this man who had been infirmed many years. We look to Jesus not some magic potions or ponds for our healing. "I am the Lord that heals you."*

John 6:2
2 And a great multitude followed Him, because **they saw His miracles** which He did on them that were diseased.

John 6:63
63 It is the spirit that quickens; the flesh profits nothing: the words that I speak to you, *they* are spirit, and *they* are **life**.

John 9:1-7
1 And as *Jesus* passed by, He saw a man who was blind from *his* birth. 2 And His disciples asked Him, saying, Master, who did sin, this man, or his parents, that he was born blind? 3 Jesus answered, neither has this man sinned, nor his parents: but that the works of God should be made manifest in him. 4 I must work the works of Him that sent me, while it is day: the night comes, when no man can work. 5 As long as I am in the world, I am the light of the world. 6 When He had thus spoken, He spit on the ground, and made clay of the spittle, and He anointed the eyes of the blind man with the clay, 7 And said to him, Go, wash in the pool of Siloam, (which is by interpretation, Sent.) He went his way therefore, and washed, and **came seeing**.

Notice it says, Jesus "saw a man". Jesus is looking out for you. He sees your struggles. He wants you to be well. Jesus made it clear that sin was not the cause of this disability. Though sin can cause illnesses and disease, in this case it was not due to sin. Sickness and disease can also be caused by addictions, environment, and other problems. If your illness is caused by your violating health standards, then you still have access to the mighty miracle working power of Jesus. God did not make this man blind so Jesus could come along and heal him. God just doesn't do things like that. There were plenty of blind people for Jesus to display His power to heal. I believe in this passage Jesus told them it wasn't because of sin that this man was blind, but that now they would see the works of God manifest in him. He wasn't saying the man was made blind so I could heal him. God never puts sickness on anyone. Why would Jesus spend so much time healing people if He didn't hate sickness so? Jesus wants you well not sick.

John 10:10

¹⁰ The thief comes not, but for to steal, and to kill, and to destroy: I am come that they might have life, and that they might have *it* more abundantly.

In this verse Jesus makes a clear statement about good and bad. The thief or the devil is here to steal from you, to kill you, and to destroy you. Are you amazed at hearing that a new disease seems to come into existence? The thief, robber, the burglar tries to steal from you. He tries to take your health. He tries to destroy your prosperity, your relationships, your passions, dreams, and every good thing God wants for you. If it's bad, it comes from the thief. On the other hand, Jesus came to bring life. He comes to bring health, prosperity, restoration, and abundant life. God brings the good. Jesus has abundant health for you. He is in no way trying to keep you from health and life. That is not who He is. He is life. Look to Jesus for your healing. And don't let the thief steal from you.

John 11:43-44

⁴³ And when He thus had spoken, He cried with a loud voice, Lazarus, come forth. ⁴⁴ And he that was **dead came forth**, bound hand and foot with grave clothes: and his face was bound about with a napkin. Jesus said to them, **Loose him**, and let him go.

Chapter 3

Healing in the Early Church

Acts 3:1-10

¹ Now Peter and John went up together into the temple at the hour of prayer, *being* the ninth *hour*. ² And a certain man lame from his mother's womb was carried, whom they laid daily at the gate of the temple which is called Beautiful, to ask alms of them that entered into the temple; ³ Who seeing Peter and John about to go into the temple asked for alms. ⁴ And Peter, fastening his eyes upon him with John, said, Look on us. ⁵ And he gave heed to them, expecting to receive something of them. ⁶ Then Peter said, Silver and gold have I none; but such as I have give I you: **In the name of Jesus Christ** of Nazareth rise up and walk. ⁷ And he took him by the right hand, and lifted *him* up: and **immediately his feet and ankle bones received strength**. ⁸ And he leaping up stood, and walked, and entered with them into the temple, **walking, and leaping, and praising God**. ⁹ And all the people saw him walking and praising God: ¹⁰ And they knew that it was he who sat for alms at the Beautiful gate of

the temple: and they were filled with wonder and amazement at that which had happened to him.

Acts 4:10
¹⁰ Be it known to you all, and to all the people of Israel, that by the name of Jesus Christ of Nazareth, whom you crucified, whom God raised from the dead, *even* by Him does this man stand here before you **whole**.

Acts 4:12
¹² Neither is there salvation in any other: for there is none other name under heaven given among men, whereby we must be saved.

Our complete wholeness—spirit, soul, and body—is found in the name of Jesus only.

Acts 4:29-30
²⁹ And now, Lord, behold their threatening: and grant to your servants, that with all boldness they may speak your word, ³⁰ **By stretching forth your hand to heal**; and that signs and wonders may be done by the name of your holy child Jesus.

The early church continued to bring healing and signs and wonders in the name of Jesus. There is no reason to think it has ever been different.

Acts 5:16
¹⁶ There came also a multitude *out* of the cities round about to Jerusalem, bringing sick folks, and them which were vexed with unclean spirits: and they were healed every one.

Acts 6:8
⁸ And Stephen, full of faith and power, did great wonders and miracles among the people.

Even Stephen, a deacon, did signs and wonders in the name of Jesus. It wasn't confined to a select few. Healing is God's idea for all the sick.

Acts 8:6-7
⁶ And the people with one accord gave heed to those things which Philip spoke, hearing and seeing the miracles which he did. ⁷ For unclean spirits, crying with loud voice, came out of many that were possessed *with them*: and many taken with palsies, and that were lame, **were healed**.

Another deacon, Philip, went about healing the sick and casting out demons.

Acts 9:33-34
³³ And there he found a certain man named Aeneas, which had kept his bed eight years, and was sick of the palsy. ³⁴ And Peter said to him, Aeneas, **Jesus Christ makes you whole**: arise, and make your bed. And he arose immediately.

Acts 10:38
³⁸ How God anointed **Jesus** of Nazareth with the Holy Spirit and with power: who went about doing good, and **healing all that were oppressed of the devil**; for God was with Him.

This is what the early church preached about the ministry of Jesus while He was here on earth. They considered this ministry continuing through the church.

Acts 14:8-10

⁸ And there sat a certain man at Lystra, impotent in his feet, being a cripple from his mother's womb, who never had walked: ⁹ The same heard Paul speak: who stedfastly beholding him, and perceiving that **he had faith to be healed**, ¹⁰ Said with a loud voice, Stand upright on your feet. And he leaped and walked.

Acts 19:11-12

¹¹ And God wrought special miracles by the hands of Paul: ¹² So that from his body were brought to the sick handkerchiefs or aprons, and the **diseases departed** from them, and the evil spirits went out of them.

Paul was not one of the original twelve disciples. He was called specifically to go to the Gentiles with the message of grace. The power of God also worked through him to heal the sick. These were "special miracles" God worked through Paul. The handkerchiefs didn't heal. God healed through the use of a handkerchief. Regardless of the point of contact, whether oil, or cloths, Jesus is the healer and healing is received by faith. Many believers are deceived into buying (giving a donation to receive) cloths or Holy anointing oil from the Holy Land. It's not the tool but Jesus who is the healer. Look to Jesus. Get to know Jesus for your healing. It's all about Him.

Acts 28:8-9

⁸ And it came to pass, that the father of Publius lay sick of a fever and of a bloody flux: to whom Paul entered in, and prayed, and laid his hands on him, and **healed him**. ⁹ So when this was done, others also, who had diseases in the island, came, and **were healed**:

The last chapter of Acts has often been called the beginning of the acts of the disciples. Where Paul left off, the rest of the church down through the ages began. Healing would be a part of that work. Until there are no sick people, there will be healing. The church, for the most part, believes this is where healing ended. But until Jesus returns, the need for healing continues. I think we the church will get what we believe. If we believe for healing, then we will carry on the work of Jesus to bring healing to the nations.

Chapter 4

Healing Teaching of the Apostles

Romans 4:16-21
[16] Therefore *it is* **of faith, that** *it might be* **by grace**; to the end the promise might be sure to all the seed; not to that only which is of the law, but to that also which is of the faith of Abraham; who is the father of us all, [17] (As it is written, I have made you a father of many nations,) before Him whom he believed, *even* God, who quickens the dead, and calls those things which be not as though they were. [18] Who against hope believed in hope, that he might become the father of many nations, according to that which was spoken, So shall your seed be. [19] And being not weak in faith, he considered not his own body now dead, when he was about an hundred years old, neither yet the deadness of Sara's womb: [20] He staggered not at the promise of God through unbelief; but was strong in faith, giving glory to God; [21] And

being fully persuaded that, what He had promised, He was able also to perform.

You are not only saved by grace through faith, your whole life is of faith so that grace may work in every area of your life. This is how Abraham lived, and he lived long before the law. He lived by the grace or favor of God. He was fully persuaded that what God said, He would perform. Nothing changed. Through Jesus we have the same promises. We, too, should be fully persuaded that anything God has promised us He will bring it to pass. He sent His Word and healed us.

Romans 8:2
2 For the law of the Spirit of **life** in Christ Jesus has made me **free** from the **law of sin and death.**

Romans 8:11
11 But if the Spirit of Him that raised up Jesus from the dead dwell in you, He that raised up Christ from the dead **shall also quicken your mortal bodies** by his Spirit that dwells in you.

1 Corinthians 11:23-26
23 For I have received of the Lord that which also I delivered to you, That the Lord Jesus the *same* night in which He was betrayed took bread: 24 And when He had given thanks, He broke *it*, and said, Take, eat: this is My body, which is broken for you: **this do in remembrance of Me.** 25 After the same manner also *He took* the cup, when He had supped, saying, This cup is the new testament in my blood: this do you, as often as you drink *it*, **in remembrance of Me.** 26 For as often as you eat this bread, and drink this cup, you do show the Lord's death until He come.

See Appendix B for more information on taking Communion for your healing.

1 Corinthians 12:28-30

28 And God has set some in the church, first apostles, secondarily prophets, thirdly teachers, after that **miracles**, then **gifts of healings**, helps, governments, diversities of tongues. **29** *Are* all apostles? *are* all prophets? *are* all teachers? *are* all workers of miracles? **30** Have all the gifts of healing? do all speak with tongues? do all interpret?

2 Corinthians 4:18

18 While **we look not at the things which are seen**, but at the things which are not seen: for the things which are seen *are* temporal; but the things which are not seen *are* eternal.

The spiritual things are even more real than the physical things we can see because the physical things are only temporary. The Word is forever, eternal. The promises of God are sure. Just look to the unseen things of God.

2 Corinthians 10:3-5

3 For though we walk in the flesh, we do not war after the flesh: **4** (For the weapons of our warfare *are* not carnal, but mighty through God to the pulling down of strong holds;) **5** **Casting down imaginations**, and every high thing that exalts itself against the knowledge of God, and bringing into captivity every thought to the obedience of Christ.

When it comes to healing, our minds will imagine all kinds of catastrophic scenarios. The battlefield of faith and doubt is in the mind. Cast down those imaginations which might plague you from fully believing for your healing. Don't let strongholds of wrong thinking and doubt take root. Renew your mind with the Word just as you are doing as you read these healing scriptures.

Galatians 3:13-14

¹³ Christ has **redeemed us from the curse** of the law, being made a curse for us: for it is written, Cursed *is* every one that hangs on a tree: ¹⁴ That the blessing of Abraham might come on the Gentiles through Jesus Christ; that we might receive the promise of the Spirit through faith.

Sickness is part of the curse. Jesus redeemed us from the curse. Jesus nailed the curse to the cross. Now we can believe the promises of God which are all Yes and Amen in Christ.

Galatians 3:29

²⁹ And if you *be* Christ's, then are you Abraham's seed, **and heirs** according to the promise.

Healing is part of our inheritance as believers. Through the death of Jesus, we have an inheritance as children of God.

Ephesians 6:1-3

¹ Children, obey your parents in the Lord: for this is right. ² Honor your father and mother; (which is the first commandment with promise;) ³ That it may be well with you, and you may live long on the earth.

Obeying in the Lord is loving. Even the Old Testament commandment had a promise of long life. But we have a greater commandment to love. Love opens the heart to peace and health. Loving your parents is one of the ways you can release health and healing to yourself and to your parents.

Ephesians 6:10-17

¹⁰ Finally, my brethren, be strong in the Lord, and in the power of His might. ¹¹ Put on the whole armor of God, that you may be able to **stand against the wiles of the devil**. ¹² For we wrestle not against flesh and blood, but against principalities, against powers, against the rulers of the

darkness of this world, against spiritual wickedness in high *places*. ¹³ Wherefore take to you the whole armor of God, that you may be able to withstand in the evil day, and having done all, to stand. ¹⁴ Stand therefore, having your loins girt about with truth, and having on the breastplate of righteousness; ¹⁵ And your feet shod with the preparation of the gospel of peace; ¹⁶ Above all, taking the shield of faith, wherewith you shall be able to **quench all the fiery darts** of the wicked. ¹⁷ And take the helmet of salvation, and the sword of the Spirit, which is the word of God:

You have the armor on if you are a child of God. Make your stand against the fiery darts of the enemy. You have the belt of truth on knowing the truth of who you are in Christ. You have your heart covered with the gift of righteousness. Your thinking is covered by salvation, and you have the sword of the Word. Therefore, stand, not letting the enemy in to confuse or vex you. Take your stand of rest in Christ.

Philippians 2:9-11

⁹ Wherefore God also hath highly exalted him, and given him a name which is above every name: ¹⁰ That at the name of Jesus every knee should bow, of *things* in heaven, and *things* in earth, and *things* under the earth; ¹¹ And *that* every tongue should confess that Jesus Christ *is* Lord, to the glory of God the Father.

At the name of Jesus, every other name must bow. Every sickness and disease that has a name must bow to the name of Jesus. Don't allow any name to take a higher place in your life than the name of Jesus. Just say that name.

Philippians 2:13

¹³ For **it is God who works in you** both to will and to do of *His* good pleasure.

Your body was created with immune systems that automatically work on your behalf. As in the natural, so the spiritual, God is at work in you to do good on your behalf. Remember His pleasure is always to heal, prosper, restore, and give you abundant life. When something happens that puts you in spiritual jeopardy, He is at work. And He is working all things out for your good.

Philippians 4:6-9

⁶ Be careful for nothing; but in everything by prayer and supplication with thanksgiving **let your requests be made known** to God. ⁷ And **the peace of God, which passes all understanding**, shall keep your hearts and minds through Christ Jesus. ⁸ Finally, brethren, whatever things are true, whatever things *are* honest, whatever things *are* just, whatever things *are* pure, whatever things *are* lovely, whatever things *are* of good report; if *there be* any virtue, and if *there be* any praise, think on these things. ⁹ Those things, which you have both learned, and received, and heard, and seen in me, do: and the God of peace shall be with you.

Don't be anxious or worried about your situation. Ask God and then allow His peace to keep your heart and mind. When doubts arise, think on the true, and good, and lovely, and pure—all characteristics of Jesus. Think on His goodness. Think on the report of the Word that you are healed and not the evil report you may have heard about your health. Let peace rule in your heart.

1 Thessalonians 5:23

²³ And the very God of **peace** sanctify you wholly; and *I pray God* your whole spirit and soul and body be preserved blameless to the coming of our Lord Jesus Christ.

2 Timothy 1:7

⁷ For God has not given us the spirit of fear; but of **power,** and of **love,** and of a **sound** *mind.*

If your are suffering from any mental problems, grab this promise that God has given you for a sound mind. Don't accept anything related to any mental problems. Don't let fear, which never comes from God, take root in your heart.

Hebrews 2:14-15

¹⁴ Forasmuch then as the children are partakers of flesh and blood, He also Himself likewise took part of the same; that **through death He might destroy him that had the power of death, that is, the devil**; ¹⁵ And deliver them who through fear of death were all their lifetime subject to bondage.

Jesus destroyed the works of the devil so that we don't have to be in bondage to fear of death. It's but a shadow to the believer. Death need not be feared.

Hebrews 4:14-16

¹⁴ Seeing then that we have a great high priest, that is passed into the heavens, Jesus the Son of God, let us hold fast *our* profession. ¹⁵ For we have not an high priest who cannot be touched with the feeling of our infirmities; but was in all points tempted like as *we are, yet* without sin. ¹⁶ Let us therefore **come boldly to the throne of grace**, that we **may obtain mercy, and find grace to help in time of need.**

Hebrews 10:23

²³ Let us **hold fast the profession of *our* faith** without wavering; (for he *is* faithful that promised;)

Hold on to the healing promises. When doubts try to creep in, begin confessing you are the righteousness of God and the healing blessings are your inheritance. You can hold on because He is faithful who gave these promises to you.

Hebrews 10:35-36

35 Cast not away therefore your **confidence**, which has great recompense of reward. **36** For you have **need of patience**, that, after you have done the will of God, you might receive the promise.

Hebrews 11:11

11 Through faith also Sara herself received strength to conceive seed, and was delivered of a child when she was past age, because she judged Him faithful who had promised.

Hebrews 12:12-13

12 Wherefore lift up the hands which hang down, and the feeble knees; **13** And make straight paths for your feet, lest that which is lame be turned out of the way; but **let it rather be healed.**

Hebrews 13:8

8 Jesus Christ the same yesterday, and today, and forever.

This is an amazing verse that reminds us that as we see Jesus in the Gospels, He is the same today. He went about healing while on earth. He is the same today. Sickness and disease have no place in the lives of His children. He cares that we are well and at peace. As Jesus is, so are we in this world (1 John 4:17). Jesus hasn't changed. He has always been and will forever be.

James 4:7
7 Submit yourselves therefore to God. **Resist the devil**, and he will flee from you.

If your are submitted to God, you are trusting Him for everything in your life. Submit the self that tries to do it and allow God to be in control of your life. When you do so, the devil won't want anything to do with you. He'll flee because He sees Jesus in you. Don't let the devil concern you. Just believe Jesus has taken care of the devil.

James 5:14-16
14 Is any sick among you? let him call for the elders of the church; and **let them pray** over him, anointing him with oil in the name of the Lord: **15** And **the prayer of faith shall save the sick**, and the Lord shall raise him up; and if he have committed sins, they shall be forgiven him. **16** Confess *your* faults one to another, and pray one for another, that **you may be healed**. The effectual fervent prayer of a righteous man avails much.

Here is another way that healing can work through the church. The prayer of faith by the elders of the church will heal the sick. They also can remind the believer that his sins are forgiven. This is especially true if they think their sickness is a result of sin. God has already forgiven their sins. Then there is the reminder that as righteous men and women, we can pray effectual prayers that really make a difference. This passage shows that we have the ability to pray for the sick and they will be healed. We can also share that our faith might be weak and we need the help of another person to pray with them. Sometimes when you are sick, pray for others and you may be healed in the process.

1 Peter 2:24
24 Who His own self bare our sins in His own body on the tree, that we, being dead to sins, should live to righteousness: **by whose stripes you were healed**.

This is Isaiah 53:5 being reiterated under the New Covenant. Jesus bore our sins on the Cross. That was 2000 years ago. So it is by His stripes we were healed. We were healed, not we may be healed or we will be healed. This is a difficult saying for most believers. We have our healing already through Jesus. We just need to appropriate it by faith. We must trust God for the healing He provided for us. Our healing is a gift of God's favor—grace. Our healing was bought and paid for by the death of Jesus.

1 John 3:8

⁸ ...For this purpose the Son of God was manifested, that He might destroy the works of the devil.

This is the purpose of Jesus coming to earth. He came to destroy, wipe out, obliterate, and evaporate the evil works of the devil including sickness and disease. The devil tried to put an iron yoke over our necks, but Jesus destroyed it. He destroyed the effectiveness of any attempt the devil might have to put sickness and disease on you. Healing is for you, not sickness. Give no place to the devil.

1 John 3:21-22

²¹ Beloved, if our heart condemn us not, *then* have we confidence toward God. ²² And whatever we ask, we receive of Him, because we keep His commandments, and do those things that are pleasing in his sight.

Our hearts should not condemn us for there is no condemnation for those in Christ (Romans 8:1). If there is condemnation for things you did or didn't do or did wrong, then it's your heart not God who is condemning you. Renew that thinking through the Word. You are not sick because of any condemnation, punishment, or wrath of God. Jesus bore it all so that you can be totally free. The commandment we keep is the commandment of Jesus to love. Love is the foundation for our salvation. God so loved that He gave. When you know that God is not condemning you for anything, you then have confidence that what you ask for you will receive. So receive your healing.

1 John 5:14-15

¹⁴ And this is the confidence that we have in Him, that, if we ask any thing according to His will, He hears us: **¹⁵** And if we know that He hear us, whatever we ask, we know that we have the petitions that we desired of Him.

Faith is simple confidence in God. It is fully believing that what Jesus did on the Cross is for your total benefit. When you are entirely persuaded then you just know that what you ask for you will receive.

3 John 1:2

² Beloved, I wish above all things that you may prosper and **be in health**, even as you soul prospers.

The Holy Spirit, through John, desires above all else that you may prosper and be in health. God wants you well. He wants you to live out your life here in peace, joy, prosperity, and health. Claim it for yourself.

Revelation 12:11

¹¹ And they overcame him [Satan] by the blood of the Lamb, and by the word of their testimony; and they loved not their lives to the death.

It's all about the shedding of blood without which there is no remission of sins. Jesus is the final sacrifice—the Lamb of God who takes away the sins of the world. Through the atoning blood of Jesus we have the benefit of healing. Keep reading the healing scriptures as you would take your daily medicine. Get them into your heart so much so that you have no doubt that God wants to heal you.

"Amen. Even so, come, Lord Jesus!" (Revelation 22:20)

Confess this every day: "I know that it's God's will for me to be healthy and well. I praise You Jesus and thank You for healing all of my illnesses, and I put my faith and trust in You."

For more encouragement or if you want prayer see www.jubileeonlinechurch.org.

Appendix A

What about going to the doctor?

Some Christians feel that if they go to the doctor, they are not acting in faith. Some groups even teach that it's a sin to go to the doctor because anything that is not of faith is sin (Romans 14:23). Many have refused their children medicine based on these beliefs. And tragically, some even die believing they are doing the right thing.

First, Jesus bore our sins on the Cross and He remembers them no more (Hebrews 10:17). Going to the doctor is not a sin. God is not going to condemn you for going to a doctor or health care facility. There is no condemnation to those who are in Christ (Romans 8:1). Love, above all else, is the right thing.

Second, I believe that any help a doctor can give you has come from knowledge that God has given the health provider community. They have a growing knowledge of methods and medicines that can really help you. I believe this all comes through the healing revelation God has given man.

Third, it is not a lack of faith to go to a doctor. Whether you go to the doctor or not, your faith is in Jesus the healer. If He uses a doctor to help you or whether He instantaneously heals you, it is Jesus who is your healer.

Fourth, use the scriptures to maximize your healing. If it isn't an emergency, take time to read the healing scriptures. Meditate on the Word. The more you go over them, the more you will sense that God is there for you. The healing verses will come alive, and you will have confidence in the healing process through the name of Jesus.

If it is an emergency, begin recalling the verses you have read. Begin speaking your healing. And as Jesus told Jairus, "Be not afraid, only believe" (Mark 5:36).

Fifth, if possible, go to a Christian doctor who can agree with you for your healing. If that isn't possible, then pray for your doctor and witness to them if the situation allows.

Sixth, when dealing with the medical community, pray that God will work through them and assist your healing. Pray for your doctors and surgeons. Pray for the nursing staff. Speak life in every situation and don't accept evil reports. You aren't denying the report, you just believe there is another report found in God's word which is more accurate.

Seventh, faith is not mind over matter; it is simply trust. Just believe that God has got your back. God loves you far more than you can possibly know. Nothing—even your unbelief—can separate you from the love of God.

Appendix B

Taking Communion for your healing.

We take Communion or the Lord's Supper to remember the finished work of Jesus on the Cross. There are two elements—the juice representing His blood, and the bread representing His body. The whole reason for Communion is to remember what Jesus did for us. Many churches have an altar carved with the word "In Remembrance Of Me."

We remember His shed blood on the cross. Through this finished work we have forgiveness of sins and eternal life through God's grace. Communion is to reflect on the death of Jesus on our behalf. Everything we have as believers is because of that one act of love.

We also remember the body of Jesus broken on the Cross for us. We are healed by the stripes on His back. So when we need healing, we can take Communion, and remember what He bought and paid for on the Cross. The elements are symbols to ignite our faith in His death on the Cross.

You don't have to wait for the once a month Communion service your church might have. You can do it as "often" as you desire. Many do it every day as a reminder of what Jesus did. You can do the same for your healing. There is Communion juice and bread available, combined in a simple cup, singly packaged for use. Many churches use them. You can buy them online or at some Christian bookstores. Take them for your healing as often as you need to take them.

Communion is not a time to reflect on your sins or if you are worthy. It has nothing to do with you, your actions, or behavior. It is only about remembering what Jesus has done. What He has done is for everyone whether they have their life "cleaned up" or not.

Also, if you don't do it right, God is not going to make you sick or kill you. This passage has been horribly misused in communion services. "[27] Wherefore whoever shall eat this bread, and drink *this* cup of the Lord, unworthily, shall be guilty of the body and blood of the Lord. [28] But let a man examine himself, and so let him eat of *that* bread, and drink of *that* cup. [29] For he that eats and drinks unworthily, eats and drinks damnation to himself, not discerning the Lord's body. [30] For this cause many *are* weak and sickly among you, and many sleep." (1 Corinthians 11:27-30)

Paul isn't talking to those believers who are taking Communion in the normal manner. No one is worthy in themselves. We are only worthy through Jesus. Many people are sick and die because they don't remember the finished work of Jesus on the Cross. They don't see that "by His stripes we were healed."

God hates sickness and disease. Jesus spent most of His time on earth healing the sick. God would never put sickness on His children nor would He ever kill someone for taking Communion wrong. Many churches put atrocious fear on people. Coming to the Communion table ought to be for whosoever and where everyone finds salvation, peace, healing and restoration.

It's not a time to examine yourselves for sin in your life. Your sins are forgiven and cast into the sea. God remembers them no more. It is also not a time to wonder if your are worthy. If you know Jesus as your Savior, you are worthy to take Communion. It is a place of safety and peace.

So never fear Communion. It's your place of healing. Take it as often as you desire. Remind yourself of the healing found in Jesus. Remind yourself that you are His child and the righteousness of God every time you take Communion. Receive your healing through the Communion.

Appendix C

What must I do to be saved?

Everyone is in one of two kingdoms. One is the kingdom of darkness which is ruled by Satan and the other is the kingdom of light which is ruled by Jesus. To get from the kingdom of darkness, where everyone starts out and in to the kingdom of light, you must be "saved" or "born-again". Salvation is much more than just "fire insurance". It is an entrance into all the blessings of God. It means being delivered from the strongholds of Satan which strangle and imprison. The way of salvation is a way of decision. You must make a personal decision about who Jesus is.

Follow these simple steps to receive salvation into your life:

> *<u>First</u>, Know that God loves you.* "For God so loved the world that He gave His only begotten Son, that whoever believes in Him should not perish, but have eternal life." (John 3:16)

> *<u>Second</u>, Know you have sinned and are eternally separated from God.* "For all have sinned and fall short of the glory of God (Romans 3:23). "The wages of sin is death..." (Romans 6:23).

> *<u>Third</u>, Know that Jesus Christ is the only way to the Father.* "Jesus said to him, I am the way, the truth, and the life; no one comes to the Father, but through Me" (John 14:6).

> *<u>Fourth</u>, Know that you must personally accept Jesus Christ as your Lord and Savior.* "But as many as received Him, to them He gave the right to become children of God, even to those who believe in His name." (John 1:12)

<u>Pray</u>: Heavenly Father, thank you for loving me and sending Jesus to die on the Cross for all my sins. Thank You for forgiving all my sins and making me righteous by the Blood of Jesus. I receive You as my Savior and make You Lord of my life.

ABOUT THE AUTHOR

God, the Father, Son, and Holy Spirit are the authors of the scriptures. The Word is alive and sharper than any two-edged sword. The scriptures stand above all other writings. They are inspired by the breath of God. Most importantly, study the scriptures.

The scriptures were compiled and the notes were added by **Jack G. Elder** who graduated from Ashland High School in Ashland, Oregon. He also received a Bachelor of Theology degree, Masters of Divinity, Doctor of Theology, and Doctor of Ministry degrees. He has pastored churches in both Southern California and Georgia. He and his wife Charlene began JubileeOnlineChurch.org—A Church without Walls Sharing God's Grace and Love—where you can read their daily devotions. You can also go to JubileeHealthPlace.org and read his diet and health articles. He is a proud husband, father, grandfather, and great grandfather. He enjoys writing, teaching, blogging, hiking, and traveling. He resides in Woodstock, Georgia.

Daily Devotions For Daily Living Vol. 2: The Riches of His Grace is our second volume of devotionals released by Amazon. Here is your opportunity to read about God's amazing grace every morning over a cup of coffee or an afternoon snack or just before going to sleep. It will build your faith as you see God's grace at work every day.

If you want to see the practicality of God's Word encouraging you to be victorious each day, seeing His goodness and blessings manifested in your life, and experiencing His Love and Grace through His New Covenant, this 365-day Word-based devotional book will be just what you need. Daily Devotions for Daily Living Vol. 2 will inspire you with the truth of God's Word for practical everyday life. It's by grace you are saved and by grace every need in your life is met.

Find it on Amazon.com.

Printed in Great Britain
by Amazon